God Is In Control

SONG BY TWILA PARIS

ZONDERVAN®

ZONDERVAN

God Is In Control
Copyright © 2010 by Zondervan

Requests for information should be addressed to:
Zondervan, *Grand Rapids, Michigan 49530*

ISBN 978-0-310-51999-7

God Is In Control
Written by Twila Paris
Copyright © 1993 Mountain Spring Music (ASCAP) Ariose Music (ASCAP) (adm. by EMI CMG Publishing) All rights reserved. Used by permission.

Cover design by Holli Leegwater | HL Design
Interior design by Holli Leegwater & Michelle Espinoza

Printed in China

09 10 11 12 13 14 15 • 20 19 18 17 16 15 14 13 12 11 10 9 8 7 6 5 4 3 2 1

God Is In Control

by Twila Paris

This is no time for fear
This is a time for faith and determination
Don't lose the vision here
Carried away by the motion
Hold on to all that you hide in your heart
There is one thing that has always been true
It holds the world together

God is in control
We believe that His children will not be forsaken
God is in control
We will choose to remember and never be shaken
There is no power above or beside Him we know
God is in control
God is in control

History marches on
There is a bottom line drawn across the ages
Culture can make its plan
Oh, but the line never changes
No matter how the deception may fly
There is one thing that has always been true
It will be true forever

He has never let you down
Why start to worry now
Why start to worry now
He is still the Lord of all we see
And He is still the loving Father
Watching over you and me

Watching over you
Watching over me
Watching over everything
Every little sparrow, every little king

God Is In Control
—How the Song Came to Be

It was an unseasonably chilly and rainy Friday morning in August in Michigan, when Twila Paris called me from her home in rural Arkansas. I expected the call but didn't know what to expect from it. Some interviewees say little while others give you the information you need without even asking. Twila proved to be one of the latter. I needed to know for this book what led Twila to write "God Is In Control." But first we exchanged pleasantries and talked about the weather, which had been quirky in other parts of the country as well.

Then with minimal prompting, Twila explained that when she wrote "God Is In Control" in the early 1990s she was "very concerned about what was going on in our nation and culture. I was beginning to feel very anxious," she said, and went on to list political and social injustices. But then, she added, "At the end of the day I always realized that no matter what people did, God was still in control."

Twila said that "God Is In Control" was written in the car, and she joked that maybe she wasn't such a responsible driver that day. She was headed to her parents' house, a 30-minute drive, and began humming. Soon the music and lyrics filled her head, and by the time she reached her destination the song was finished. And

as she finished telling me this she began sing-ing it softly into the phone—my own private concert!

I had the information I needed, and so we turned to talking about the state of the world today. She told me that following 9/ll a lot of concert tours were being cancelled but she decided to keep her schedule intact. At one performance, she planned to sing the national anthem and considered asking the audience to join in, but then decided not to. But when she started singing the audience rose and began singing with her anyway. "I start to choke up whenever I tell this," she said. It was clear that she felt that whatever happens in our world, ultimately everything will be all right. And it was even more clear that she truly believed that the reason was because God is indeed in full control.

Steven Cole

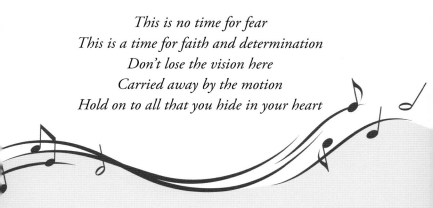

This is no time for fear
This is a time for faith and determination
Don't lose the vision here
Carried away by the motion
Hold on to all that you hide in your heart

My heart is steadfast, O God, my heart is steadfast.

Psalm 57:7

Create in me a pure heart, O God, and renew a
steadfast spirit within me.

Psalm 51:10

The God of all grace ... will himself restore you and
make you strong, firm and steadfast.

1 Peter 5:10

There is one thing that has always been true
It holds the world together
God is in control

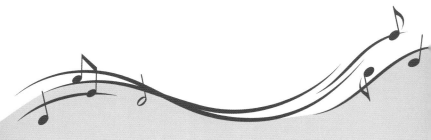

He is the Lord; let him do what is good in his eyes.

1 Samuel 3:18

For the Lord spoke, and it came to be;
he commanded and it stood firm.

Psalm 33:9

All public power proceeds from God.

Pope Leo XIII

We believe that His children will not be forsaken
God is in control

God governs the world; the actual working of his government,
the carrying out of his plan, is the history of the world.

Georg Hegel

The LORD your God goes with you; he will
never leave you nor forsake you.

Deuteronomy 31:6

The LORD loves the just and will not forsake his faithful ones.

Psalm 37:28

We will choose to remember and never be shaken
There is no power above or beside him we know
God is in control

Say to God, "How awesome are your deeds! So great is your
power that your enemies cringe before you."

Psalm 66:3

Praise the LORD ... He has shown his people
the power of his works.

Psalm 111:1,6

Blessed is the man who fears the LORD ... his
heart is steadfast, trusting in the Lord.

Psalm 112:1,7

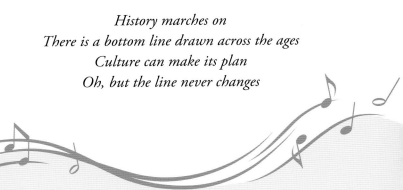

History marches on
There is a bottom line drawn across the ages
Culture can make its plan
Oh, but the line never changes

Everything God does will endure forever.

Ecclesiastes 3:14

Give thanks to the LORD … his love endures forever.

1 Chronicles 16:34

God's righteousness endures forever.
2 Corinthians 9:9

No matter how the deception may fly
There is one thing that has always been true
It will be true forever

He is the LORD our God; his judgments are all in the earth.
He remembers his covenant forever, the word he
commanded for a thousand generations.

Psalm l05: 7-8

Dominion belongs to the LORD and he rules over the nations.

Psalm 22:28

God rules forever by his power, his eyes watch the nations.

Psalm 66:7

He has never let you down
Why start to worry now?

He rescued me from my powerful enemy, from my foes, who were too strong for me. They confronted me in the day of my disaster, but the LORD was my support.

2 Samuel 22:18-19

Your love, O LORD, supported me. When anxiety was great within me, your consolation brought joy to my soul.

Psalm 94:18-19

The LORD says, "I am he who will sustain you."

Isaiah 46:4

He is still the Lord of all we see
And he is still the loving Father
Watching over you and me

The Lord will keep you from all harm—he will watch
over your life; the Lord will watch over your coming and
going both now and forever more.

Psalm 121:7-8

From heaven the Lord looks down and sees all mankind;
from his dwelling place he watches all who live on earth.

Psalm 33:13-14

The Lord who watches over you will not slumber.
Psalm 121:3

Watching over you, watching over me
Watching over everything

The Lord is faithful, and he will strengthen and protect you from the evil one.

2 Thessalonians 3:3

The LORD protects the simplehearted.

Psalm 116:6

Does he who formed the eye not see?

Psalm 94:9

Every little sparrow, every little king

The eyes of the LORD are everywhere, keeping watch
on the wicked and the good.

Proverbs 15:3

God Is In Control

SONG BY TWILA PARIS

ZONDERVAN   ♫ Music